Navigating Grief

10 Simple Tips to Overcome Loss

Chuck Carr

Navigating Grief
10 Simple Tips to Overcome Loss
Written by Chuck Carr
Copyright©Chuck Carr 2020
All Rights Reserved 2020

Cover design and photo by Chuck Carr
No part of this publication may be reproduced, transmitted in any form (electronic, mechanical, photocopying, recording, or otherwise) without prior written permission of the copyright owner.

Send inquiries and letters to the author to:
Chuck Carr
P.O. Box 241
Crabtree, Pa 15624

For more information, blog topics, and other books, visit:
Chuck-Carr.com

First Printing: May 2020

Scripture references are taken from the ESV Bible Scripture quotations are from the ESV® Bible (The Holy Bible, English Standard Version®), copyright © 2001 by Crossway, a publishing ministry of Good News Publishers. Used by permission. All rights reserved.

Contents

Introduction: 7

Day 1: 15
Day 2: 21
Day 3: 27
Day 4: 35
Day 5: 39
Day 6: 45
Day 7: 51
Day 8: 57
Day 9: 61
Day 10: 65

Closing: 69

Navigating Grief

10 Simple Tips to Overcome Loss

Chuck Carr

Introduction

     Grief. It is a mystery. It is a natural certainty. To grieve, is to be human. To be human, is to grieve. The strongest and smartest minds can't fully understand it. Many try to uncover secrets about it, yet its pattern doesn't fit every mold the same exact way. We can study it, but it expresses itself differently in each person it overtakes. It lasts different lengths of time; it plagues some much longer than others. Grief does not always play by the rules.

     Grief. As a massive black sky looming over your head, grief is the endless cloud of despair that seems to show no relief in sight. It is a great choking blanket of darkness, and it doesn't show favoritism. To the young, the old, the rich, and the poor alike, it stalks us, not partial to any one race, gender, or nationality. Grief will coat any soul over with thick despondency. No matter where you live, how many friends you have, or the color of your skin, it will haunt the one who flees from its clutches.

     Grief. As a dreadful task master demanding allegiance, it forces one to swallow the hard bondage of suffering and affliction. Voluntarily or not, it drafts slaves up to obey its forced bidding, and then locks them in a prison without windows. One cannot escape it by simply changing physical location. There is no fooling it, hiding from it, or making deals with it. Grief is a monster all to itself.

Grief. An identity, one who is dressed in black. Grief will not ask permission to inhabit, become, or take over. It will steal one's name and rob one's character. Grief desires to replace all the good in a person with darkness. It stops for nothing. A blackened name of dirt and grime, it varnishes one over with a glaze of shame. Grief changes everything. Although it mimics the character and nature of a person that once used to be, like a puppeteer, it controls everything anew. Grieving people are not themselves. Grief is a false form of identification, one formed and fashioned in a dark basement of clouded judgment. One's likes, preferences, emotions, and countenance are all changed at its whim and pleasure.

Grief. It is the pain inside, the hurt that one cannot expose for who and what it is. It is a longing for more of what never can be obtained. It is the realization of broken dreams and destroyed hopes, replaced by sadness and hurt unwanted. It is the reminder of what has been lost. It is a continually dripping faucet, filling and overflowing a bucket of sorrow.

Grief. What a word. It is sometimes acute and shocking, sometimes sudden. Grief can take without warning, like an unanticipated stab to the heart. Other times it can be seen coming from afar, sometimes even expected, as an hourglass watched for the last grain of sand to fall. One thing grief is not? It is never desired.

Grief. It is a liar. Cold thoughts and words once believed will force the strongest retreat, backing into a cave of self-isolation and self-focus. The liar is bold. The liar tells you that you are all alone. The liar insinuates that nobody else will understand. Bridges are burned as the lies are believed; social walls and boundaries are set up that are unhealthy and unnecessary. The liar wins by betraying truth, forging confidences of clear vision, and posing as imposters of sound advice.

Grief. Sometimes it is an enemy. Sometimes it is a friend.

If you are reading this, chances are you are searching for something to help you cope with a loss you have experienced in life. That is basically what grief is: the struggle to cope with the emotions associated with the loss of someone or something that is valuable to you. Most commonly, people associate grief with the passing of a loved one. It brings emotions and thoughts to the forefront, as you now have to cope with the absence of someone you once loved in your life. But grief doesn't stop there.

There are many things that can cause grief, not just death. Divorce can cause grief. When the heart bleeds for a dream that seemed so perfect but ended in shambles, we grieve the loss of a beautiful future. People grieve the loss of time spent with children when a family splits in two and time must now be shared. One can grieve the loss of a job. One can grieve the loss of financial stability. Health issues are another thing that people often grieve from. Accidents or disease can bring changes in one's physical or mental health, and serious grieving can occur with these unwanted health losses.

Whatever the reason for grief, big or small, it is valid if you are feeling the negative emotions and thought patterns that come with grief.

I also know that many times people do not *want* to get better from grief. Things may still be too raw, too deep, or too fresh for someone to be able to take any steps to help get through the process. That was where I was when my first wife passed away in 2008. I didn't want to feel better. I didn't want to be comforted. It hurt too bad. I stayed in that place for a long time. People tried to tell me things, clichés of sympathy, and it only made me more upset. I had too many unanswered questions. I had too many emotions too close to the surface. I had to process things first. If that is you, my heart goes out to you. It is never easy.

My intentions of this booklet are to help you make grief manageable. I will never claim these tips to take grief away. To be honest, grief never goes away. I will forever bear the hurt and scar inside my heart for the loss of my first wife. I have come to the place in my life that I can acknowledge that although it hurts, and I know it won't ever stop, I can still continue living my life in the victory and calling that Jesus has purposed me to be. I can do it with a smile on my face. God has an abundant life for me to live. Yes, it was tragic. But no, I don't have to wear ashes for the rest of my life. God has made it possible for me to look back in my past, enjoy and savor the moments we shared, and keep living with a smile. Whether you have lost a loved one, your health, a job, or some other form of loss, the tips outlined here can help you still continue living, even living rather well. If you are struggling with living under the burden of grief, the simple tips included within this writing will help you navigate through it, making the most of your quality of life as you cope with your loss. I do admit that grief is complicated, and sometimes messy. It is not always clear cut and simple. What works well for one person may or may not necessarily be the golden ticket for someone else. These things helped me though, and I would be pleased to share them freely with you. I know it is hard. My intentions are to help you see that God's hand is still open to you, and there can be joy there when you come to him.

Although I am not a professional, I do have "real-world" qualifications to what I am talking about. I have been qualified both by trial, and by my confession of faith, as 2 Corinthians 1:3-4 clearly states:

> Blessed be the God and Father of our Lord Jesus Christ, the Father of mercies and God of all comfort, who comforts us in all our affliction, so that we may be able to comfort those who are in any affliction, with the comfort with which we ourselves are comforted by God.

Without going into too much detail, I have suffered plenty of losses in my lifetime. Each one was unique to itself. When I was hit with these traumatizing losses, I learned quite a few things about what worked and what didn't work. In my memoir titled *All That the Locusts Have Eaten*, I go into much more detail about the losses that I have been forced to face in life. Losses are not fun. Nobody wants to have losses. But thank goodness you don't have to stay shackled in your grief. It is possible to learn how to successfully *live*, despite going through grief. You can overcome the losses. Although these losses will never go away, God didn't design you to be a defeated person walking around with your head down and wearing a black cloud all your life. He wants you to live the life abundant. I'm just one voice who can testify that it is true.

How does one help him or herself through the stages of grief? It is easier said than done. It is important to realize that healing is a process, and not an instant fix. My hope for you in reading this, is that you can take these simple steps and tips and apply them to your life. If you give them an honest try, I believe that you will see the benefit from them. I truly want you to be able to cope with your grief. I truly want you to live the abundant life that God has for you. In this booklet, I have made an outline of ten practical steps that a grieving person can use to help overcome grief, or be victorious in wrestling with it. They are simple things that helped me when I was in desperate need of something to grab hold of. Please, only focus intentionally on one each day, so you don't take on too much at one time. You need to be in this for the long haul and taking time to lay a good foundation will be much more beneficial than sprinting to the next step unprepared. If you struggle with a step and need two days to process it, then so be it. Take the time that you need to do things well. Continue working through this booklet until the end. When finished, repeat the steps all over again until they become habitual or engrained inside you.

Over time, you will slowly start to do these things without realizing it. One day you will wake up and the pain will not be as bad. When that happens, the monster named grief won't be so intimidating, and with God's help, you will be able to live an abundant life despite your loss.

You are more than a conqueror.

May God bless you and bless your journey.

Chuck.

Day 1:
Find a Solid Supporter.

    This tip is a must. Trust me, you do not want to go through grief alone. Grief is like a bandit. If you don't watch out, it will chew you up and spit you out. Grief will rob you blind. It has no qualms about lying to you, telling you that nobody out there cares, nobody wants to help you, and sooner or later that you are all alone. When you are in the heat of the battle, and grief smacks you square in the face, most people feel that they are exactly that... alone.

    Whether a grieving person admits it or not, time, space, and reality are all twisted and contorted when you are in the midst of grief. Reality is skewed. Facts are bent. Eyesight is not clear. The *reality* of your true situation might be that there are supporters in every direction, but through the lenses of your clouded and grieving glasses, you can't see any of them. I know this because I've been there. I thought I was all alone. I was in a bad place. Others told me that I wasn't seeing clearly, that help was around me, but I didn't believe them. Now that I'm on the other side, I understand how wrong I was. There is a lot more help available to you than what you think.

    Grief tends to isolate us. Isolation is closely tied to depression. Depression further isolates us deeper. It is a brutal and ongoing cycle of pain. To be honest, when you are grieving, you don't want to be around anybody, but that is exactly what you need. You need a support group. You need a few friends or siblings or whoever you trust to be there for you. Some days you will need an ear to vent to. Some days you will need advice. Some days, you will need your support team to slap you in the face and say "wake up, look at what you are doing!"

    The mind is drastically altered and effected by grief. Everything about how you think and reason, gets all scrambled up and put back in a different order than what it used to be in. It is very wise to have a solid connection to at least one other close and trusted person, so that when you start to make irrational decisions, they can help steer you back on the right path. When I lost my first wife, Becca, people kept telling me not to make any big decisions right away. It irritated me. I didn't want to hear that. I thought I was fine. Why? Because grief clouds your judgment so heavily that you can't even tell it is off focus. I thought I was perfectly capable of rational thought, and consequently, made some pretty big financial decisions too quickly.

    A grieving mind isn't ready to handle big decisions yet, because it is easily distracted by panic and fear. Panic and fear are the tag-team that drive our irrational decisions, cloaking them as sound choices. Looking back, I've made some pretty goofy decisions early on, and now know they were fear based or panic driven. For instance, when my wife died, I was afraid to use any of her cooking utensils for fear that I would break or wear them out. I went out and bought a whole new kitchen so as to protect her things and keep her alive in my mind. A kitchen is the most expensive room in the house, and I racked up quite a charge in buying all new cooking equipment. At the time it seemed perfectly logical. Now, I see it a little differently. Looking back, I probably didn't need to buy to such an extent, as there is little sentimental value in silly things like a wire whisk. I went crazy because I was afraid. Yes, some things were worth saving. But I didn't need to buy *everything* new.

      I have heard suggestions on the length of time needed for one to prolong big choices and may or may not agree with them. I don't think there is a set amount of time that works for everybody. I think true friends are the best indicator of when a person is healed enough to carry on with resuming life choices once again. A true friend wouldn't let someone get hurt, make poor choices, or fall into unhealthy coping strategies. Solid supporters not only help you when you want them to, they help you when you don't.

      Find a support system. Link together with a few good friends. Talk to those who have gone through grief before. Have people available for the moments that you are going to break down and not know what to do. Have a "meltdown plan" or "strategy" in place. One example of this is when I put into practice driving to social gatherings myself. I would never carpool. When attending social outings, family parties, or other group events in which I may have felt a little worried or uncomfortable with, I would drive my own vehicle. In my mind, it was a great escape plan. If I had a meltdown or was triggered, I wasn't trapped in a situation without a car to get out. Having a plan gave me confidence to attend, because I could leave at any time I wanted to. Another plan I had in place was a go-to babysitter for when I was emotionally overwhelmed. I had my parents close by and I could drop of the boys in a safe and cared for place anytime I needed fresh air. I knew I could count on my parents to be there at a moment's notice, and that was a huge help as a lifeline of security. It gave me a stable platform on which I could have the courage for growth and healing.

The better your safety net is, the less likely you will be trapped, caged, or caught in hard situations. Put in place a team that you can run to and trust. It is vital. Don't attempt to face grief on your own.

Scripture Help:
Ecclesiastes 4:9-12
Two are better than one, because they have a good reward for their toil. For if they fall, one will lift up his fellow. But woe to him who is alone when he falls and has not another to lift him up! Again, if two lie together, they keep warm, but how can one keep warm alone? And though a man might prevail against one who is alone, two will withstand him—a threefold cord is not quickly broken.

Action Steps:

Who can I trust and depend on to help me through my grief?

How can I connect with that person(s) in a healthy way so that I have a support system in place under me?

Do I have a strategy in place when the meltdown of an unexpected trigger occurs?

How can I contact that person today?

Day 2:
Get Out the Crock-Pot.

This one is a no-brainer. Seriously, we all need to eat. When I first faced being a single dad, Becca left me with two beautiful boys, ages five and three. With that tremendous blessing, also came tremendous work as one person's responsibility. I was swamped. We had needs, real ones, and they all needed attended to. One of the biggest life hacks that I found to prove helpful was the suggestion by a friend to purchase and use a crock pot. I already had one, but now began to use it more. It was a fantastic suggestion.

Everybody likes a hot, home-made meal, but most of us rarely have the time or energy to put into making one. If you are a grieving single mom or dad, this is an essential life hack. There are thirty-thousand other things demanding your immediate attention throughout the day. Socks need paired and folded. Laundry needs done. Kids need to have baths, and teeth need to be brushed. If you are a grieving single, you still have demands, and they are stressful. Your job or career demands compete with the demands of a grieving and healing soul. In both situations, there seems to be no limit to the job list. Everything under the sun needs done, it all needs finished now, and there is no way you have enough time and energy to get it all accomplished.

To keep your sanity and your health, try using the crock-pot to simplify your life. Since grieving causes your brain to be overly used in other ways besides planning ahead for meals, you can throw frozen things in too, making planning simpler. You don't need to fret that you forgot to get a meal out of the freezer to thaw- just throw it in frozen. You can throw raw things in, whole things in, anything in. It simplifies wash and clean-up time, as you don't need to cook things in other pots and pans before combining it to the rest of your meal. There are a ton of good crock-pot cookbooks out there. Pick some up. You can use tried-and-true recipes or you can use your imagination. I even tried dumping uncooked rice, beans, canned tomatoes, and peppers into a crock-pot so we could enjoy bean burritos. No matter what you like to eat, it can almost all be done in a crock-pot.

Think of it... it's easy! No pots and pans to wash or cooking utensils to clean.

To take it even a step further, several companies sell crock-pot liners. I cook like a pirate, doing as little as possible to get the job done. Don't judge, I had way too much to do. I don't want to do anything that causes extra work later on. Sometimes I don't exactly follow the specific ingredient measurements just because I don't want to wash another spoon. When I got my first order of crock-pot liners, I thought I had found the golden ticket. It is a game changer. I highly suggest it.

When less time is spent on cooking and cleaning, you get more time to enjoy doing other things. Mealtime conversations and discussions will be of higher quality because you won't be exhausted from cooking. You won't get discouraged when you *"slaved all day cooking"* only for your family to *"gobble it all down in an instant."* Family time will be of higher quality. Social times for singles will be better too. When guests and friends come over to support you, you won't need to spend extra energy by cooking. You will have time to do the things you love. After-supper moments will be much more relaxing.

On another note, you will be filling your body with better nutrition. Cooking with a crock-pot means using more whole foods and less prepackaged or processed cardboard. You will be giving your body the fuel it needs to get through the stress at hand. The stress of grieving puts higher nutritional demands on your body. If you fuel it right, you will have more energy, and feel better. Crock-pots are a win-win.

Scripture Help:
Matthew 6:25-34
"Therefore I tell you, do not be anxious about your life, what you will eat or what you will drink, nor about your body, what you will put on. Is not life more than food, and the body more than clothing? Look at the birds of the air: they neither sow nor reap nor gather into barns, and yet your heavenly Father feeds them. Are you not of more value than they? And which of you by being anxious can add a single hour to his span of life? And why are you

anxious about clothing? Consider the lilies of the field, how they grow: they neither toil nor spin, yet I tell you, even Solomon in all his glory was not arrayed like one of these. But if God so clothes the grass of the field, which today is alive and tomorrow is thrown into the oven, will he not much more clothe you, O you of little faith? Therefore do not be anxious, saying, 'What shall we eat?' or 'What shall we drink?' or 'What shall we wear?' For the Gentiles seek after all these things, and your heavenly Father knows that you need them all. But seek first the kingdom of God and his righteousness, and all these things will be added to you.

"Therefore do not be anxious about tomorrow, for tomorrow will be anxious for itself. Sufficient for the day is its own trouble.

Action Step:
Obtain and put into practice the regular use of a crock-pot to simplify meals. If money is not an issue, sometimes this suggestion can be replaced with ordering take-out, or some other form of making less work (like using paper plates).

What things can I do during supper preparation to ensure that I can enjoy the rest of my day?

If you don't have a crock-pot, where can you obtain one?

How many, and which days of the week will be my crock-pot days?

What menus can I create for crock-pot days?

What cookbooks do I need to buy to make life simpler?

Day 3:
Run into God, not away from Him.

    For many people, this is the hardest tip on the list, and it will require the most effort. That is one reason why I didn't put it first on Day 1. I figure we need to get some forward momentum and start the ball rolling before tackling this giant issue. Now that you have a solid support team in place and a crockpot simplifying your meals, we can take a deep breath and face a bigger challenge.

    When a person loses a loved one, especially one in which they had spent a lot of time in prayer asking for a healing, they can very easily become indignant towards God. When I was forced to face grief in 2008, I admit that I had a beef with the Lord. It is only natural to a human in a fallen world, but many people try to hide their feelings from God, almost pretending their emotions towards him don't exist. They keep living a plastic imitation of what the real relationship looked like before the loss occurred, fooling everyone except God and themselves. I was one of them. At the time I was a youth pastor, and people like that (church leaders) are expected to have all the answers to hard questions, right? Did I have faith? Yes. Did I pray without ceasing? Yep! I did everything that you are supposed to do when you are looking for answered prayer. My wife and I went to church. We got the elders of our church to pray over her and anoint her with oil. We even had massive prayer chains of people who were faithful to pray for a healing. An army was beside us. Everyone trusted for a miracle, not a death.

But God didn't answer things that way.

In my book titled *The Convergence*, Weston Tanner had a similar issue. He faced the "why's," those nagging and plaguing thoughts and questions that rob you of inner peace and comfort. *Why didn't God heal my wife? Why did Brooklyn have to die? Why do bad things happen to good people? Why didn't God answer my prayer?* These types of questions and many more flood the mind of the person who is waist deep in grief. You know what? Sorry to disappoint you, but many of these questions will remain unanswered this side of heaven. We don't know why things happen the way they do. To get to its simplest form of nuts and bolts, we live in a fallen world. When Adam and Eve bit into that forbidden fruit, everything changed. Sin ushered death into the earth, and bad things have been happening to good people ever since. We know from the book of Isaiah that God's ways are higher than our ways and his thoughts are higher than our thoughts. I know that doesn't sound like a very good answer to the person who just lost a loved one, but God ultimately *does have* things in his control, and he answers our prayers in ways we don't understand sometimes. No matter what happens, even if tragedy occurs, God can orchestrate something good out of something horrific. There is nothing a fallen world can do to you that God can't take and turn around for good. There is nothing a fallen world can throw your way that God can't take and make beautiful. He is redemptive. Goodness is his nature.

I also go into this subject in descriptive detail in my memoir *All That the Locusts Have Eaten*. Without giving away a spoiler, I want you to know that God's redemptive power can flow to the lowest valley, bringing a hurting person back to an abundant life. It is possible, and this book of mine testifies to it.

What are my suggestions to dealing with the "why's?" It is plain and simple. Get them out.

One day while buried in unresolved grief and anguish, I had a mentor give me one of the greatest pieces of advice in my life. In a phone conversation with him, he explained very simply that I cannot keep holding onto my burdened feelings. I was counseled to get my feelings out, even if that meant telling God how mad I was at him. I had so much bottled up inside. I was upset with God; he was supposed to rescue me, not leave me high and dry. I felt like my life was in shambles because he didn't stand up to heal. I couldn't help but feel a certain level of blame towards him. I know this is not going to sound very spiritual, but I was in an ugly place. I needed to beat on God's chest, and my mentor knew that. He told me to go outside, where nobody could hear or see, and get all the penned-up frustration off my heart and onto his. He advised me that God was big enough to handle it. I listened to my mentor tell me that I didn't need to worry about telling God what I felt inside, even if it sounded like it might hurt him. He promised me that when I was done blowing off my steam, God would put his arms around me like a gentleman and embrace me in his love, and I would feel better. Then, we would have restored relations.

What did I do? I went out into the woods where I could yell and scream and swear and get it all out without anybody watching or hearing. I punched my truck, denting it. I found a metal pipe and started smashing tree branches and such. I started telling God what I felt, even if a curse word slipped out now and then. I let him know how upset I was with him. He hadn't done what I wanted. I trusted him. I put all my hope in his name. I felt let down. I pounded hard on his chest and got it all out.

When I was finished screaming, I was exhausted. Emotionally and physically, I was whooped. I slumped down beside my truck and cried. I sat there a broken man, sitting shattered, and in pieces.

A very beautiful thing then happened.

God met me. He held me all together. He not only was big enough to handle everything I just screamed and yelled, but he loved me enough not to leave me in that awful place. He wasn't offended. He wasn't hurt. He wasn't surprised. He cradled me in his enveloping love of mercy and grace. There were no walls between us anymore. He had listened to what I had to say. Now that my anger was all out, we could commune with each other in intimacy. It was one of the most special moments of our entire relationship. I was broken into tears. He held each one.

Why do we feel like we have to pretend with the Lord? What does the Bible say? I challenge you to read the entirety of Psalm 44. In it, David does a very similar thing. He asks the Lord the hard questions. He doesn't hide them. He tells God exactly what he feels. That is the first step to restoring your walk with the Lord. If you never come face to face with these emotional conflicts, there will always be an invisible and unspoken wall between you and God. Unless you truly release the blame from off God's shoulders and address this conflict, you will go around and around in a cycle of tension. Your relationship with God won't mature. It will become stagnant, going nowhere.

If you are someone who is plagued with the "why" and "how" questions, you need to get them all out. Pretending your feelings are not there won't do you any favors, you will only ruminate things causing more pain and delayed victory. You don't have to be dignified. You don't have to look or act like everything is fine and dandy. Tell God exactly what you feel so you can move into a restored relationship with him again. Don't run away from God. Run into him. He is the only source of lasting comfort, and you won't find true peace outside of his arms.

Scripture Help:
Psalm 44:9-26
But you have rejected us and disgraced us
and have not gone out with our armies.
You have made us turn back from the foe,
and those who hate us have gotten spoil.
You have made us like sheep for slaughter
and have scattered us among the nations.
You have sold your people for a trifle,
demanding no high price for them.
You have made us the taunt of our neighbors,
the derision and scorn of those around us.

You have made us a byword among the nations,
a laughingstock among the peoples.
All day long my disgrace is before me,
and shame has covered my face
at the sound of the taunter and reviler,
at the sight of the enemy and the avenger.
All this has come upon us,
though we have not forgotten you,
and we have not been false to your covenant.
Our heart has not turned back,
nor have our steps departed from your way;
yet you have broken us in the place of jackals
and covered us with the shadow of death.
If we had forgotten the name of our God
or spread out our hands to a foreign god,
would not God discover this?
For he knows the secrets of the heart.
Yet for your sake we are killed all the day long;
we are regarded as sheep to be slaughtered.
Awake! Why are you sleeping, O Lord?
Rouse yourself! Do not reject us forever!
Why do you hide your face?
Why do you forget our affliction and oppression?
For our soul is bowed down to the dust;
our belly clings to the ground.
Rise up; come to our help!
Redeem us for the sake of your steadfast love!

Isaiah 55:8-9
For my thoughts are not your thoughts,
neither are your ways my ways, declares the Lord.
For as the heavens are higher than the earth,
so are my ways higher than your ways
and my thoughts than your thoughts.

Proverbs 18:10
The name of the Lord is a strong tower;
the righteous man runs into it and is safe.

Action Steps:
In what ways am I blaming God for my loss?

Be honest with yourself and God. Have I hidden my emotions from the Lord? If so, how can I get things off my chest in a healthy way? Talk to him. Let him listen. Then listen to him.

Write out a letter to God, expressing your emotions, giving them to him, and releasing him from any blame you have put on his shoulders.

Day 4: Do Things You Enjoy.

    This might sound like common sense, but when we are in the middle of grieving, we can easily "forget" to do things that bring us enjoyment. When the burdens and blanket of hard grief covers over you, the temptation to retreat into a corner of doom and gloom is very strong. It is only natural. Many people get so entangled in this place of despondency that the "taste" for formerly enjoyed things don't seem salty anymore. If one goes into this dark place and follows that train of thought, he or she can become trapped in their own created room of despair. Doing things that you enjoy, (even if you don't "feel" like doing it at the time), will protect you from this kind of isolation.

    I know what you are going to say. It can be very hard to start this step. Maybe due to the loss of a loved one you are *afraid* to enjoy things in life. Maybe you feel that if the person you lost can't enjoy doing those things, then you shouldn't either. Maybe you feel that some things were special to the both of you, and now that your loved one is gone, you feel *guilty* for enjoying something. Maybe you feel guilty for enjoying anything *period*. Maybe you feel like you have to *punish* yourself so that guilty feelings don't arise. This is why you have to be intentional about doing enjoyable activities even if you don't *feel* like it.

The first time you try to do something enjoyable, it is going to be very hard. Awkwardness may make you uncomfortable. Getting your mind to allow you to take action might feel like pulling teeth. You may run into horrible feelings, triggers, or snags. But if you push through, the second time will be a little bit easier. Just like someone recovering from post-traumatic syndrome, intentional, little steps will lead to improved health. Over time, doing things you love to do (or loved to do in the past), will become an avenue of expression, one that provides a lifeline for you in which you can go to for a physical and mental battery charge in a sense. Your energy can be expressed. Your passion can be expressed. Your creativity can be expressed. Whether it is reading a book, climbing a mountain, going kayaking, watching movies, going out to eat, gardening, drawing, or playing sports, doing something that you enjoy is going to give you relief when you need it while putting a smile on your face. As long as it is a healthy choice for an activity, go for broke. Laugh. Smile. Enjoy.

Scripture Help:
Romans 8:1-2
There is therefore now no condemnation for those who are in Christ Jesus. For the law of the Spirit of life has set you free in Christ Jesus from the law of sin and death.

Action Step:
What are five things I like to do, and how can I do one of those things today?

1)

2)

3)

4)

5)

What plan of action will I have in place, so that if I get triggered into fear and anxiety or guilt about doing these things, I can carry though and reach my goals?

Day 5: Splurge on Yourself.

When I was going through grief, I somehow fell into the rut of being so concerned with taking care of everybody else that I forgot to take care of myself. I had kids that needed fed, clothes that needed washed, bedtime stories that needed read, and of course, I still had a job to show up to and function at. There were a million-and-one things to do each and every day. All my energy, resources, and time were spent on, and for, other people. The person stuck in this unfortunate place of being a single parent with children can easily get burned out. If you are not careful, even with the best intentions, the demands of life and responsibility of caring for others will quickly snuff you out. I found this out the hard way. I tried to be that superhero single parent who could master balancing everything all at one time. I did everything well... all except taking care of myself.

You know how every time you sit down in an airplane seat aboard a commercial flight you must listen through the same speech about the safety procedures of the aircraft? We hear the warning each and every time we take a flight, yet we never practice what is said. When the oxygen mask drops in the moment of an emergency, who is supposed to put on their mask first? That's right, you. If you don't put on your oxygen first, how are you going to be able to assist in helping other people?

I thought I could go about my days without taking care of me. I was the last person I felt I needed to invest my attention in. Bzzzzz. Wrong answer! Incorrect. Go to jail. Do not pass go. Do not collect two hundred dollars. If you are not intentional about taking care of yourself, you will burn out and fizzle into the wall flowers faster than you think. As into it and engaged as your heart might be, you cannot take care of other people long term without taking care of yourself. It is that simple.

If you really want to be successful in taking care of others, you absolutely MUST take care of yourself. Eating healthy, exercising, keeping yourself in tune spiritually with God, having a good support team for emotional needs, and getting enough sleep are all essential things that a grieving caregiver must do to keep themselves in the game. Trying to shortcut yourself only will make you crabby, irritable, and temperamental, all while robbing you of much needed energy. You can't afford to short yourself. You can't afford to be snippy and quick tempered with those around you either.

One thing that helped me was journaling. During my grief, I would wake up early before the boys got up and make myself a really nice hot cup of coffee. Adding my favorite cream, I would then sit and pen my thoughts. It was something that kept me alive during the crazy years I spent grieving while also trying to raise two kiddos. Maybe it sounds crazy to you, but I needed time to sit still, and sitting still became my favorite thing in the whole world to do. It could recharge me unlike anything else, and it became essential that I sat still so that I could handle the rest of my day. I would go to Barns & Nobles, and splurge on expensive Italian hand-designed leather journals. It felt good to hold such a high-quality item in my hands when I spent time doing what I loved. By writing in them, I could say whatever I needed to say. I could speak all my frustrations. Combining it with another passion of mine, coffee, the delight was blissful. I could enjoy the sips of steaming hot Irish Crème coffee, relishing in the flavor and aroma. I would treat myself to something special, like a special blend or expensive variety of beans. Though this might seem small or insignificant, I worked hard enough during my days juggling a career and a family together, and I felt splurging on my favorite coffee and cream was an indulgence I had earned. It felt good.

      Other things that people might try are buying a new pair of running shoes, getting a gym membership, splurging on going to your favorite restaurant, or getting some new music to listen to. The list is endless and the possibilities are totally up to your own style and creativity. Find out what works for you.

Scripture Help:
Matthew 7:3-5
Why do you see the speck that is in your brother's eye, but do not notice the log that is in your own eye? Or how can you say to your brother, 'Let me take the speck out of your eye,' when there is the log in your own eye? You hypocrite, first take the log out of your

own eye, and then you will see clearly to take the speck out of your brother's eye.

Action Step:

Within a reasonable budget, what are some things that I have put off that would bring me enjoyment if I allowed myself to indulge in them?

Have I shorted myself in ways that if I made a purchase or indulged in something, I would have more jump to my step when I take care of others? What will I allow myself to enjoy and splurge on myself today with?

Day 6: Let Yourself Grieve.

It is my opinion, but I strongly hold it to be true, that those of us who *allow* ourselves to grieve are far and away better off than those who suppress feelings of loss and act as if they do not exist. I have seen people who experience terrible losses and move right into tomorrow as if nothing ever happened. Again, it is my opinion, but this type of mentality will not permit a person to progress forward in life in the long run. It will come back to bite. When people ignore their feelings of loss, it tends to resurface down the road in inopportune moments of time, sometimes when you least expect it, or in an ugly way you don't anticipate. It could trigger a meltdown during a professional job. It could cause difficulties with other relationships around you, such as family members that you care about. It could break or blow up future relationships down the road. If nothing else, resisting the grieving process prevents you from having closure, robbing your heart of inner peace. God wants you to have peace. It is ok to grieve.

When I grieved, I grieved hard. It wasn't pretty, it wasn't dignified, but in the end, it worked for me. I am able to say that the way I grieved allowed me to move in steps that would bring myself to an abundant life in the future, and I don't have many regrets about what I did. Everybody grieves differently. One of the ways I chose to grieve was trailing the two-year-long medical journey that my wife and I walked all over again. I went to each of the hospitals that we went to for treatment. I went to the chemotherapy treatment center. I took pictures of the rooms she stayed in, the beds she laid in, the chairs I sat in while being with her. I traced the path over again, eating the same food in the cafeterias, drinking the same coffee like I once had. I even went to the hospital chapels again that I had once gone seeking the Lord for a healing. These places seemed to be even more special now. I soaked the sights and sounds in a second time.

Some people might think this is a bit morbid, but to me, it was very beneficial to my health. From the very beginning of our bout with cancer, we savored the doctor visits and hospital times as "dates." Since we were already forced to be there, we took advantage and made the most of our time together. Our doctor dates shared very good times, not just bad. Some of the greatest bonding moments we ever had together as a married couple were in some of the ugliest places, and when I went back to those places, I could feel the love again I longed to keep and hold onto. Some of the nurses that had treated my wife would talk to me, even doing simple acts of kindness for me that made big differences. A sympathetic nurse gave me a hospital gown to cherish. They seemed to understand. For my health, it was a journey that I had to take. I would have someone watch the boys, then would drive off to Pittsburgh, Latrobe, Greensburg, and seemingly a thousand other places just to rest in the aura of the good times I remembered.

Does it sound crazy?

Do it anyways.

Who really cares what other people think? If you need to drive to a hospital so you can drink Seattle's Best coffee and eat a breakfast sandwich, go for it. If seeing light shining in one particular hospital hallway window reminds you of a moment of connection with God when you prayed for your loved one, then do it again. Grieving doesn't need to make sense to someone else. It is *your* thing. *Your* way. *Your* time. You can do it how *you* need to. As long as it isn't something unhealthy, or detrimental to you or someone else's health or property... it's fair game. Go for it.

I strongly advise each and every person who reads this to permit themselves to grieve, in whatever natural and organic way grief presents itself in. If your loved one had a favorite restaurant, eat there for their birthday. Do what you both always did for your anniversary. Go back to that special place that only the two of you know about. Take a pack of gummy bears to their gravestone. Plant their favorite flowers. Do whatever you need to do, and do it well. You will thank yourself later. Grieving requires that you heed it. When you do, you can one day look back and smile instead of cry, enjoy the memories instead of dismissing them. Don't worry, you will never forget that special loved one; he or she will always have a place inside of you. But now when you do remember them, it will be a memory of love and satisfaction. Even Jesus permitted Himself to grieve. He once lost a very dear friend. In that, His soul was deeply troubled. He didn't just cry, but in fact, he wept.

Scripture Help:
John 11:32-35
Now when Mary came to where Jesus was and saw him, she fell at his feet, saying to him, "Lord, if you had been here, my brother would not have died." When Jesus saw her weeping, and the Jews who had come with her also weeping, he was deeply moved in his spirit and greatly troubled. And he said, "Where have you laid him?" They said to him, "Lord, come and see." Jesus wept. So the Jews said, "See how he loved him!"

Action Step:
In what ways have I not permitted myself to grieve? How would it help me if I allowed myself to grieve?

I give myself permission to grieve today. If I cry, I cry. Today is a day in which it is ok to feel the pain of loss.

Day 7:
Get Fresh Air.

Even the best of us get overwhelmed sometimes. Grief can consume. It's like a fire that never seems satisfied, always hungry for more. It doesn't ask if you are willing to give, or if you are wanting to obey it. It takes way more than you want to allow, and like a hungry dog, it will keep begging for more. Grief has a bottomless appetite.

When we become overwhelmed, *which will happen*, we need an exit strategy in place to keep our sanity. To be honest, a *prevention* strategy is even a better choice. Everybody needs some good, old-fashioned, fresh air from time to time. If you put into practice taking a moment or two to step out of your situation, you will be able to stand tall enough to fight it when you step back in.

I was an ice hockey player in high school and college. One of the fundamental principles of the game is the management of line changes. You can have the most talented star in the world on your team, but if you don't manage his lungs and legs, you won't get far. Tired legs don't skate well. Being out of breath doesn't score goals. Instead of skating around the rink like a waltz, a coach demands hustle. Get out on the ice. Give it one hundred and ten percent. Bust your butt, skating your hardest. Then get back to the bench and let someone else do the same while you recharge. Fresh legs win games.

The same is applied to grief. Every once in a while, you must get off the ice to catch your breath so that you can return to the game more effective and ready. If you don't, you are not only hurting yourself, but hurting the whole team.

I think that men and women understand this concept differently from one another. I believe there is a God-wired need that our creator designed and put into the brain of a man to "disconnect" from things temporarily. That is why men are so good at shutting the world out while you watch your favorite sports team on a Sunday afternoon or sitting on the stream bank waiting on a big fish to bite. Men open one window at a time, achieve the task at hand, and then close it. Men can effectively shut out the world and recharge by doing "nothing." Women on the other hand, tend to be wired by God to simultaneously orchestrate fifty things at a time, with half-opened windows in each room of the house. Unlike men, women are especially gifted to be able to do "many things," and might have a hard time momentarily shutting off. It might be very difficult for a woman to put things out of her mind and take a break from a stressful grieving situation. To you women in my audience, you may have to be extra intentional with this step. My best wishes go out to you.

Although a woman might find it harder to do this than a man, men and women both need to take a time out from the duties and obligations of caretaking and other work accumulated from grieving to breathe some fresh air. It could be in the form of gardening, going for a car drive, taking a walk, or going to a park. It doesn't have to be something huge, just something intentional. I experienced this one day when I almost snapped from being overwhelmed.

The two-year battle with cancer that my late wife faced was trying on the whole family. Those of you who know my situation personally, know that I took the upmost care of her while she was sick. I actually feel like I did rather well; mentally I was able to keep my head in the game so that I could provide the best care possible for her. But one day in particular, for whatever reason, I felt a sudden strike of panic flash through me. I was grieving the loss of her health, even before she passed away. It was very difficult for me to watch her health decline.

It wasn't any noteworthy day of struggle. It was just an ordinary day, the same as all the rest. She was getting a sponge bath, and I had to put new pain patches on her. I don't know why, but for some reason that day bothered me specifically. It broke me down to see her so frail and hurting. It triggered something inside me; I was very pained to see the condition of our situation. I had to go jogging. I needed air like a choking victim.

The run wasn't anything out of the ordinary either. It was just a jog up the road and around the countryside like many of the other runs that I frequently went on. But on that day, in that moment, I needed air. I needed to step out of my situation. I allowed myself to unplug from the caretaker mode I was in and plug myself into something else so I could recharge. It was only about two or three miles, but when I got back, I was mentally equipped to handle things once again and was able to step back in to effectively aid her. Without it, I wouldn't have been able to help her or myself.

You might be in a similar situation. Maybe you are grieving someone's health and they are still alive to tell of it. Maybe someone has passed away and now you are left with a thousand responsibilities. Maybe you lost your job. Regardless of the loss you are suffering, it is important to intentionally take a quick break now and then so the grief of the matter doesn't consume you. If you don't, you'll burn out. If that happens, you won't be able to help anybody.

Jesus gives us a great example of how one needs to recharge. Even the Son of God in human skin needed time away to recharge His batteries.

Scripture Help:
Matthew 14:22-23
Immediately he made the disciples get into the boat and go before him to the other side, while he dismissed the crowds. And after he had dismissed the crowds, he went up on the mountain by himself to pray. When evening came, he was there alone,

John 6:22-25
On the next day the crowd that remained on the other side of the sea saw that there had been only one boat there, and that Jesus had not entered the boat with his disciples, but that his disciples had gone away alone. Other boats from Tiberias came near the place where they had eaten the bread after the Lord had given thanks. So when the crowd saw

that Jesus was not there, nor his disciples, they themselves got into the boats and went to Capernaum, seeking Jesus.

When they found him on the other side of the sea, they said to him, "Rabbi, when did you come here?"

Action Step:
What are healthy ways for me to get outside and breathe some fresh air?

How can I schedule some "air times" throughout my week to prevent burnout?

Day 8:

Exercise.

This suggestion is vital. The sooner you can get exercising the better. It is almost an instant fix. In the most simplistic of terms, grief causes stress and is detrimental to the body. Exercise relieves stress and is edifying to the body. Therefore, exercise is a good remedy for grief.

Without going into a whole bunch of science, what happens when we exercise? I would like to list some commonsense benefits from exercising during the grieving process, ones we can all agree upon even without a science degree.

More than likely when you decide to exercise, you are going to get out of your normal four-walled room and go somewhere else, right? Your surrounding changes. You go to the gym. You go outside. Wherever you go, it is different from where you are. You choose to enter a different environment. That, is a very good thing. Getting out gives you a chance to free your mind from the rut of an environment that reminds you most of your misery. Changing the scenery is healthy and fresh.

No matter if you like to be alone or like to be with people, exercise can be accommodated to suit. Exercise can be a solo thing for introverts who like to think deep inside while they work out. Exercise can also be a together thing for extroverts who feed off the energy of others. Whatever your personality, your mind is able to renew itself when you physically exert, with or without other people.

Exercise increases your heartrate in a healthy way. It is good to physically work your heart. Anxiety is taxing on your heart, a negative burden that tightens it up with panic and fear. To work your heart without those emotions is much healthier and better for you.

Exercise is a way you can track yourself for positive improvement. If you can walk the hill this week, maybe you can jog the hill next week. In four weeks, maybe you could run right up and over it. The self-noted and trackable advances in your progress will give you confidence in something, and that something will be positive. The achievement of something noteworthy and worked for will heighten you above the stress of grief.

One great thing about exercise is that you can vent your feelings while doing it. Are you frustrated? Take it out on the weights in the gym. Use a punching bag. Use it as a coping mechanism for the emotions you don't know how to process. Are you tired? Increased activity in exercise will give you more steam throughout your week. You will start to feel more energy and less fatigue over time.

Finally, physical exertion chases away the depressing blues of grieving. Regardless of why, when we exercise, our body begins to pump and move, and when that happens, the blues begin to leave. It is very hard to stay depressed throughout a good workout. The body is simply designed to be in a better mood when we put it through the rigor of exercise.

Scripture Help:
1 Corinthians 9:24-27
Do you not know that in a race all the runners run, but only one receives the prize? So run that you may obtain it. Every athlete exercises self-control in all things. They do it to receive a perishable wreath, but we an imperishable. So I do not run aimlessly; I do not box as one beating the air. But I discipline my body and keep it under control, lest after preaching to others I myself should be disqualified.

Philippians 3:12-14
Not that I have already obtained this or am already perfect, but I press on to make it my own, because Christ Jesus has made me his own. Brothers, I do not consider that I have made it my own. But one thing I do: forgetting what lies behind and straining forward to what lies ahead, I press on toward the goal for the prize of the upward call of God in Christ Jesus.

Action Step:

What exercise plan is right for me? How can I begin to (realistically) begin to exercise? Start small and gradually work up to higher things. What activities would help me in exercise?

Plan out a weekly schedule of exercise and stick to it. You will feel significantly better.

Day 9:
Aim to Complete a Project.

    I really like to shoot archery. I have a pretty high-quality compound bow and am passionate about the sport. Before the accident that changed my life, I was very engaged in shooting frequently and set up a shooting range at my house. I set a target up, a plastic wrapped round bale of straw. It is great for shooting long distance because it is so big (five feet by five feet), and that prevents you from losing arrows by missing. I generally practiced from sixty yards. I would hang my bow from a hook on our kids' treehouse before going to retrieve my arrows. Archery is a great pastime.

    This might sound obvious, but if I didn't spray paint a target onto the big-bale backstop, I couldn't expect to become a better archer, right? It's not likely to happen without a focal point. But, as soon as I took a paint can and sprayed a red dot in the center, everything changed. I then had something to aim for. I had something to focus on. When I would draw my bow string back and take aim to shoot, the only thing I would then see was that little-red dot. Everything else faded away.

    Having a goal is a great piece of advice for someone who is grieving. In the same way as shooting arrows at a target, your attention and focus can be pinpointed to accomplishing something productive, and the awareness of the grief around you will diminish and fade in comparison. We've heard the phrase "aim small, miss small," taken from various movies. Basically, the gist of the saying is that if you aim at a big target (like the whole bale) and miss, you miss the whole target. If you aim at something little on the target (like the bullseye) and miss, at least you still hit what you are shooting at. Having the goal of completing a project is the same. To make the point even clearer, when I became good at shooting sixty yards, then I would move back to seventy. When I accomplished what goal I had, I could move back farther and practice at a more difficult distance. You always can improve. You always can reach for a new target. Make a different goal. Take aim. Shoot.

Find something specific and be detailed about it. If you like reading books, set a goal to read 30 books in one year. If you want to want to restore an antique car, then set a date that it has to be finished by. Write down the details of what your goal will look like if you accomplish it. Know ahead of time what an accomplish goal will look like and don't settle for anything less. Attach a due by date to the project and post it someplace visible. Get someone else to hold you accountable.

When my life started to go out of control back in 2006, my late wife was undergoing chemotherapy treatments. During that time period of my life, I felt like there were so many things *out of control* that I needed at least one thing to *still be in control*. I decided that one thing to be my weight. I set a goal. I wanted to weigh one-hundred-seventy-five pounds.

I knew what I wanted to see when I stepped on the scale, and each night I checked my weight, almost religiously. Even though my life was spinning into chaos, each time I stepped on the scale to watch the needle move, I was able to watch something that I had control over. It gave me a focus. I had something to work to and aim for. If I was above the mark, then I was self-disciplined enough to eat better and exercise more. I now had full control over at least one element in my life. It was one thing that I alone could determine the outcome of.

It helped tremendously.

My challenge is for you to find something similar that you can do for yourself. We are challenged in the same way spiritually from God's Word.

Scripture Help:
Matthew 6:33
But seek first the kingdom of God and his righteousness, and all these things will be added to you.

Matthew 7:7-8
"Ask, and it will be given to you; seek, and you will find; knock, and it will be opened to you. For everyone who asks receives, and the one who seeks finds, and to the one who knocks it will be opened.

Action Step:
What target could I set up to aim for? What goal or project can I aim to complete?

Write out what your goal is in detail, post it in a visible place, and take steps in aiming for it. Don't stop until you achieve the goal.

When you do achieve it, set up a new target for something harder and take aim again.

Day 10: Take Care of Someone Else.

This is one that most people don't think of but is a great life hack. When we take care of someone else who is in a similar unfortunate situation, the focus instantly comes off of our own problems and becomes tuned into the positive things we are doing in another person's life. There may be no greater way, no way so satisfying, that helps you through the grieving process.

Sometimes the most overwhelming part of grieving is that we can't take our eyes off of it. It is everywhere we look, and plagues everything we do. It surrounds, consumes, and overtakes us. You might be in that place right now, a place so engulfed in grief that it seems impossible NOT to see it. It might follow you all day. Though you try to shake free from it, grief never stops dragging close behind. When grieving hit me hard, I couldn't shake it. It was right beside me when I woke up. It went to the kitchen when I went down to eat breakfast. When I went to work, it came along uninvited. At lunch it hovered over me. At the end of the workday, it met me at my front door. Grief went everywhere I did, all day long. Grief is an unwanted shadow.

Is there a person in your neighborhood who is in a rough situation? Is there someone else that needs a hand? By coming to the aid of that person, you not only find fulfillment in life with the good you do for them, but your own problems will seem to disappear. I have done this multiple times throughout my life. When things get heavy, and the weight of the world burdens you down, help someone else lift their burden. Their troubles might actually seem extremely light and easy to manage. Other people's problems and grief are much easier to dissect and pick apart, view objectively, and their problems are easier to come up with concrete solutions for because you are not engulfed in their emotional mix. You can see clearer through someone else's grief than your own. Beside's that, it feels good to help people. Feeling like you mattered to someone else, bringing someone relief, being stable for someone when they are weak, and cheering someone up are all positively charged activities. Helping someone else helps ourselves. The good feeling inside will carry you through your day. It won't only bring benefits to the receiver of your actions, but the positive thoughts and emotions will begin to help heal your own heart and mind as well. Healing is a long journey. Helping others on the way makes the journey much more bearable.

It isn't fun to be down in the dumps all the time. Doing something for someone else is an escape, a symbiosis that brings blessings to both parties.

Scripture Help:
Galatians 6:2
Bear one another's burdens, and so fulfill the law of Christ.

Action Step:
Who in my sphere of influence needs my help right now?

What can I do for that person to make their life of higher quality today?

Closing

There are few things in life as complex and controlling as grief. A soul suffering loss either willingly or unwillingly succumbs to its presence and power. We were created as beings meant for relationships. When we break that apart and unpack it, there are two important ones to keep in mind. Jesus teaches on these two things.

> Matthew 22:34-40
> But when the Pharisees heard that he had silenced the Sadducees, they gathered together. And one of them, a lawyer, asked him a question to test him. "Teacher, which is the great commandment in the Law?" And he said to him, "You shall love the Lord your God with all your heart and with all your soul and with all your mind. This is the great and first commandment. And a second is like it: You shall love your neighbor as yourself. On these two commandments depend all the Law and the Prophets."

The very thing that grief can attack the worst is the thing that we need to protect most fervently. Jesus tells the Pharisees what is most important in life. Relationships is what life is all about. Our relationship with our Heavenly Father is the greatest relationship we will ever have or know. Second to it is the relationship we have with our fellow brother and sister in humanity. Grief tries to destroy both of those bonds. Although grief is natural and expected to come knocking on the door in our fallen world, hopefully this booklet will give you some concrete ways to preserve your relationships and manage the process while it is occurring.

Grief is hard. There is no easy way around it. But you do not have to do grief alone, and you don't have to let go of God's hand while going through it. He is more than there for you. If he walked along side me in my grief, he can victoriously guide you through it as well. My thoughts and prayers go out to you as you navigate through grief. Grief can destroy, but healing repairs.

And healing is what I hope you may find.

May God bless you on your journey.

With God, there is always hope.

Romans 8:28

Other titles written by Chuck Carr:

The Convergence
Where Tragedy + Hope Collide
Fiction Novel
February 2020

Learn more about Life Compass Ministries
At:

Chuck-Carr.com

Facebook.com/AuthorChuckCarr

Letters to the author can be sent to:
Chuck Carr
P.O. Box 241
Crabtree, Pa 15624

Or

Paintwaves7@gmail.com

www.ingramcontent.com/pod-product-compliance
Lightning Source LLC
Chambersburg PA
CBHW071032080526
44587CB00015B/2582